Being in Government

So You Want to Be a
U.S. SENATOR

by Kassandra Radomski

Consultant:
Fred Slocum,
Associate Professor of Political Science,
Minnesota State University, Mankato

CAPSTONE PRESS
a capstone imprint

Fact Finders Books are published by Capstone Press
1710 Roe Crest Drive, North Mankato, Minnesota 56003
www.mycapstone.com

Library of Congress Cataloging-in-Publication Data
Names: Radomski, Kassandra, author.
Title: So you want to be a U.S. senator / by Kassandra Radomski.
Other titles: So you want to be a US senator | So you want to be a United
    States senator
Description: North Mankato, Minnesota : Capstone Press, [2020] | Series: Fact
    finders. Being in government. | Audience: Ages: 8 to 9. | Audience:
    Grades: 4 to 6.
Identifiers: LCCN 2019004860| ISBN 9781543571950 (hardcover) | ISBN
    9781543575293 (paperback) | ISBN 9781543571998 (ebook PDF)
Subjects: LCSH: United States. Congress. Senate—Juvenile literature. |
    Legislators—United States—Juvenile literature. | Vocational
    guidance—Juvenile literature.
Classification: LCC JK1276 .R34 2020 | DDC 328.73/071023—dc23
LC record available at https://lccn.loc.gov/2019004860

Editorial Credits
Mari Bolte, editor; Jennifer Bergstrom, designer;
Jo Miller, media researcher; Laura Manthe, production specialist

Photo Credits
AP Images, 29, (Bottom); iStockphoto: Steve Debenport, Cover; Newscom: Congressional
Quarterly/Scott J. Ferrell, 17, CQ Roll Call/Tom Williams, 15, 27, Everett Collection, 13
(Top), Jeff Malet Photography, 10, KRT/Chuck Kennedy, 13 (Middle), MCT/Dennis Drenner,
20, Polaris/CNP/Ron Sachs, 24, Pool via CNP/Andrew Harrer, 29 (Top), Pool via CNP/
Olivier Douliery, 19, Roll Call Photos/Tom Williams, 23, SIPA/Alex Edelman, 16, UPI/Bill
Greenblatt, 9, ZUMA Press/Ann Parry, 13 (Bottom); Shutterstock: Andrea Izzotti, 12 (Top),
Everett Historical, 12 (Middle), 12 (Bottom), JPL Designs, 7; Wikimedia: Scrumshus, 5

Design Elements
Capstone; Shutterstock: primiaou, Rebellion Works, simbos

All internet sites appearing in back matter were available and accurate when this book was
sent to press.

Printed in the United States of America.
PA70

TABLE OF CONTENTS

WANTED:
U.S. SENATOR

Do you like meeting new people? Is it your dream to help others solve their problems? Can you give inspirational speeches to raise money or convince people to agree with you? Have you ever been curious about what a senator does? If you answered "yes" to any of these questions, then becoming a senator may be for you!

Requirements for Being a Senator

There are three requirements for this job. They are spelled out in the United States Constitution.

To become a senator, a person must be:

✓ at least 30 years old

✓ a U.S. citizen for at least 9 years

✓ a resident of the state where they seek election.

Senators work at the U.S. Capitol Building in Washington, D.C. Construction began in 1793 and Congress used the building for the first time in 1800.

Senators are elected for a six-year term. After that, they can run again. Candidates should be willing to work—many senators work more than 40 hours per week. Completing high school is essential. A college degree is strongly recommended. Many members of Congress are lawyers, which means they have both a college degree and a law degree.

GET ALL
THE DETAILS

The U.S. government is made up of three parts: the **legislative**, **executive**, and **judicial** branches. The legislative branch makes the laws. The executive branch carries out the laws. The judicial branch interprets the laws. The Senate and the House of Representatives are part of the legislative branch. Together, the Senate and House are known as Congress.

The main responsibility of senators is to participate in making laws. They also decide how the federal government's money is spent. They spend time talking to people in their home states about important issues. Then they bring those concerns to the U.S. Capitol in Washington, D.C.

Senators confirm high-ranking appointees in the executive branch and federal judges, including Supreme Court justices. They also have the power to remove government officials suspected of wrongdoing.

★ THE ★ THREE BRANCHES OF GOVERNMENT

LEGISLATIVE
Makes Laws

EXECUTIVE
Carries Out Laws

JUDICIAL
Interprets Laws

 Congress

 House of Representatives

Senate

 President

 Vice President

 Cabinet

 Supreme Court

 Other Federal Courts

CONSTITUTION
created the three branches

executive branch—to do with the branch of government that makes sure the laws are obeyed

judicial branch—the part of government that explains laws

legislative branch—the part of government that passes bills that become laws

FACT: Since the first election of 1788 and through the end of 2018, 1,974 men and women have been elected to and served in the United States Senate.

Getting Elected

Each state elects two senators. Until 1913 state **legislators** elected senators. The Founding Fathers planned it that way. They did not trust everyday people to make the best decisions about who should represent them in government.

Having state legislators elect senators had one big flaw. It made it easier for senators to intimidate or **bribe** legislators for their votes. And if the legislators couldn't agree on senators, Senate seats stayed empty for months. Sometimes states didn't have full representation in Congress for years. Other times, arguments over open seats led to legislators refusing to work in protest. This meant laws could not be passed at the state level.

Finally, in 1913, the 17th Amendment was passed. This gave all citizens the right to vote directly for their state's senators. This is the system we use today.

FACT: Like Congress, most state legislatures are made up of two chambers, or houses, called the Senate and the House. Nebraska is the only state that does not have two houses. Its legislature is unicameral, meaning it has only one house.

Debates are one way voters can get to know more about the candidates running for Senate seats.

amendment—a change made to a law or a legal document

bribe—giving money or gifts to persuade someone to do something

legislator—a person elected to make or propose laws

Senator Krysten Sinema was sworn in by vice president Mike Pence in 2019.

Senators serve six-year terms. About one-third of all senators in the United States are up for re-election every two years. Senators from the same state are elected in different election years. It is designed this way so there is the opportunity for new and experienced members to serve at the same time. The new senators elected in 2018 will serve from the beginning of the 116th Congress on January 3, 2019, to the end of the 118th Congress on January 3, 2025.

Political Parties

Political parties are made up of like-minded people who run in elections and pass laws. The main political parties in the United States are the Republican Party and the Democratic Party. Senators, representatives, and the president are members of a political party. To run for office as a member of a political party, each needs to be **nominated** by the party. Some candidates run as independents, without a party nomination.

RE-ELECTED ...AGAIN!

Senators can run for election as many times as they want. Twenty-five senators have served for 35 years or longer. Robert Byrd, a senator from West Virginia, was re-elected eight times between 1959 and 2010. He served for 51 years, 5 months, and 26 days. Hawaii's Daniel Inouye served for nearly 50 years.

FACT: The **majority party** is the political party with the most senators or representatives. The **minority party** is the political party with the fewest senators or representatives.

majority party—the party whose members make up more than half of the total membership of the group

minority party—the party whose members make up less than half of the total membership of the group

nominate—name someone as a candidate for a government position

Senate Timeline

Declaration of Independence

James Monroe
(1758–1831)

Hiram Revels
(1827–1901)

JULY 4, 1776: The Declaration of Independence is approved; it is signed on September 17.

1788: The Constitution is ratified; the first elections take place; Robert Morris and William Maclay from Pennsylvania are the first senators elected.

MARCH 4, 1789: The first Congress meets in New York City.

1816: James Monroe is the first former senator to be elected president.

1870: Hiram Revels becomes the first African American elected to represent Mississippi.

1922: Rebecca Felton is sworn in as the first woman senator. She was appointed to fill a vacant position; she served for one day.

1932: Hattie Caraway is the first woman elected to the Senate.

1948: Margaret Chase Smith is the first woman to serve in both the House and the Senate.

1992: Carol Moseley Braun is the first African American woman elected to the Senate.

2001: Hillary Clinton is the first "first lady" to be elected senator; she was still serving as first lady when she was sworn in.

2018: A record number of women—25 senators—are elected to Congress.

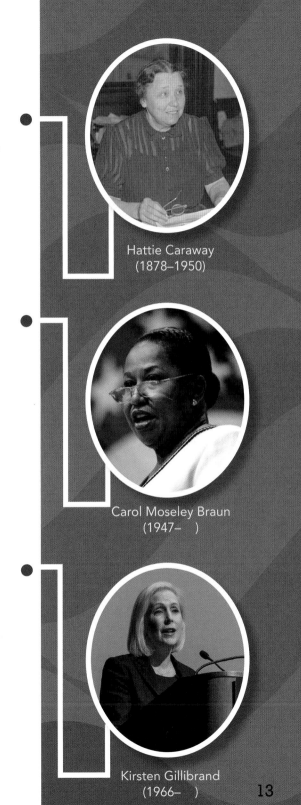

Hattie Caraway
(1878–1950)

Carol Moseley Braun
(1947–   )

Kirsten Gillibrand
(1966–   )

Chapter 3

MAKING LAWS

Senators spend a lot of time learning about issues faced by people in their states. Sometimes those concerns become bills. Some of those bills become laws. Senators must work together, along with House members and leaders, to write, discuss, and pass bills.

Senators also discuss **appropriations** bills. These bills involve decisions about **federal** taxes. They also include spending for federal government agencies and programs. Appropriations bills must start in the House of Representatives. Then the House and Senate must agree on them before they can be sent to the president.

The senator who introduces the bill to other senators is the bill's sponsor. The bill is then sent to a committee and possibly a subcommittee. Senators talk about the bill, research the issue, and make any needed changes. Then they vote to approve it. Then it either goes back to the Senate floor for more discussion or to another committee for their approval.

There are 20 permanent Senate committees and four joint committees, which are made up of both House and Senate members. Each committee has its own staff, funding, and rules.

FACT: Each bill is given a name and a number. Bills that start in the Senate are named with an S. Bills that start in the House of Representatives begin with H.R.

appropriations—the congressional power to collect taxes and authorize spending federal government money

federal—relating to the U.S. government

EVERYONE SEES

Congressional bills may be seen by multiple committees. Subcommittees focus on how the bills apply to more narrow areas of policy. Assigning a bill to one or more committees or subcommittees is called referral.

First the committees approve the bill. Then it needs to be approved by at least 51 senators. Finally, it is sent to the House of Representatives. It goes through a similar process in the House. If representatives make changes to the bill, then senators must agree to those changes. If they don't, the senators and representatives must reach a compromise.

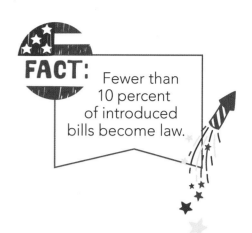

FACT: Fewer than 10 percent of introduced bills become law.

Texas senator Kevin Brady, chair of the Ways and Means Committee, announced the Tax Cuts and Jobs Act in 2017.

NONSTOP

Senators discuss issues on the Senate floor. Representatives are limited to how long they can debate, but senators can talk as long as they want. There is nothing stopping a senator from talking for hours to block a bill. This is called **filibustering**. To stop a long filibuster, at least 60 senators must vote to end it. This is a process known as **cloture**. Former Senator Strom Thurmond holds the record for his 1957 filibuster. It lasted 24 hours and 18 minutes.

When a law is passed by the Senate and signed by the president, it becomes a law and is known as an Act of Congress.

After passing through both the House and Senate, the bill goes to the president. The president will either sign or veto it. If the bill is signed, it will become a law. If the bill is vetoed, it goes back to Congress. However, if at least 67 of the 100 senators and 290 of the 435 representatives override the president's veto, it can still become law.

cloture—a procedure for ending a debate and taking a vote

filibuster—an effort to prevent action by making a long speech

Chapter 4

WHAT ELSE DO SENATORS DO?

Senators have many responsibilities. They divide their time between the U.S. Capitol and their home state.

There are three office buildings in Washington, D.C., used for Senate business: the Russell, the Dirksen, and the Hart. Each has offices for senators, meeting rooms, cafeterias, and room for support staff. People can schedule a tour through their senator's offices. They can also arrange personal meetings to talk about issues that are important to them.

Some of a senator's time must be spent meeting with other senators. Sometimes all 100 senators meet. Other times a group of senators meet in a committee or subcommittee. There, they draft, discuss, and revise bills. Then they decide which ones will go to the Senate floor. The Senate is not in session every day. Some weeks they may meet twice. Other weeks, they might meet all five weekdays. On average the Senate has met 162 days a year since 2001.

A tunnel and subway link the Russell Senate Office Building to the U.S. Capitol Building. There is a similar transportation system between the Dirksen and the Capitol. The Hart is the farthest away and is connected by a train.

FACT: According to the Constitution, Congress needs to meet at least once a year. There are no other guidelines on how many days its members should meet.

Even if they're not in Washington, senators are often working. One study showed that members of Congress work about 70 hours a week while in Washington, D.C., and 59 hours a week at home. Nearly 80 percent of Congress members spend more than 40 weekends a year in their home states. And some have a long commute. In 2012 Senator Mark Begich traveled 10 hours every week to get from Alaska to D.C. Hawaii's Senator Brian Schatz spent around 20 hours traveling each week. However, some senators don't go back and forth much at all.

Senator Amy Klobuchar holds "Minnesota Mornings" in her Washington, D.C. office every Thursday the Senate is in session. Visitors can meet the senator and enjoy coffee and pastries.

Some senators spend their time at home learning about new bills, attending fundraisers or press conferences, or meeting with their **constituents**. Minnesota Senator Amy Klobuchar visits all 87 counties in her state every year. Former Delaware senator and vice president Joe Biden was famous for his train rides to and from Washington, D.C.

OTHER PERKS

On top of a D.C. office and a nice paycheck, senators receive other job perks. Some include:
> allowances for staff, office supplies, and travel
> life, death, and health insurance
> staff to help schedule events, research issues, and work with constituents
> lifelong **pension** after retirement (depending on age and length of service)
> reserved parking spots at airports in Washington, D.C.
> access to a private gym and dining room
> access to the House or Senate floors even after the senator's term is up

constituents—the people who live and vote in a Congress member's home state or district

pension—money paid regularly to people who have retired from work

Enforcing the Law

Senators play a part in making the laws. They are also responsible for upholding them. Senators have the power to remove an official from office. An official can be **impeached** if he or she is suspected of committing serious crimes or acting improperly. Two presidents, one Supreme Court justice, 15 federal judges, and a war secretary have faced impeachment.

IMPEACHMENT

Forcefully removing an official from office is rare. Since the Constitution was put in place more than 200 years ago, the House of Representatives has impeached only two presidents. Neither was convicted by the Senate. Of the 15 federal judges impeached by the House, only eight have been convicted and removed from office by the Senate.

Federal Judge G. Thomas Porteous (center) was impeached and removed from office in 2010. His charges included accepting bribes and making false statements under oath.

The House of Representatives must vote for impeachment. Then the Senate decides whether that person is innocent or guilty. At least 67 senators must vote yes for an official to be removed from office.

impeach—charge an elected official with a serious crime; it can result in removal from office

Confirming Appointments

The president nominates members to his or her Cabinet. Members of the Cabinet advise the president on different areas of policy. The president also nominates people for many executive branch positions, some military positions, federal judges, and Supreme Court justices. The Senate must approve the president's nominations. Usually this goes smoothly. However, sometimes the nominees are not approved. In 2016 Republican senators refused to vote on President Barack Obama's Supreme Court nominee, Merrick Garland. This left a Supreme Court position open for more than a year.

Vice President Joe Biden (left) watched as President Barack Obama nominated Merrick Garland (right) on March 16, 2016. Republican senators would not grant a Senate hearing for Garland.

Approving Treaties

The president can negotiate **treaties** with foreign governments. At least 67 senators must also vote in favor of them. Sometimes treaties are rejected by the Senate. The president then has the option of changing the treaty and trying again to get approval.

Keeping Order

The Constitution gives senators the right to discipline other senators for disorderly behavior. This usually means a formal statement of disapproval, rather than removing a senator from office. Since 1789 only 15 senators have been expelled. Fourteen supported the Confederacy during the Civil War. The last was charged with conspiracy and treason. Only four have actually been convicted of crimes.

treaty—a formal agreement between groups or nations

SENATE LEADERS

Do you like to lead others and help organize activities? Then perhaps one of the Senate's leadership positions is for you.

Senate Leader

The vice president is the ceremonial leader of the Senate. Even though this sounds like a powerful position, he or she is rarely even present during Senate sessions. If there is a vote that is tied 50 to 50, the vice president casts the tiebreaking vote.

President Pro Tempore

The president pro tempore is elected by the Senate. He or she is usually the longest continuously serving senator from the majority party. If something happens to the president, vice president, and the Speaker of the House, then the president pro tempore is next in line to be president. The person in this position lets senators know when it is their turn to speak. They make sure there is order in the Senate.

Senate majority whip John Thune in 2019. He was elected senator in South Dakota in 2004 and elected majority whip in 2018.

Majority and Minority Leaders and Party Whips

These leaders speak about their party's position on issues. The majority leader represents the party with the most senators. The minority leader represents the party with the fewest senators. Each party's senators elect their leader at the beginning of each session of Congress. The party leaders serve two-year terms. They can keep their roles and be re-elected as long as the majority party does not change.

The majority and minority leaders get help from the majority and minority party whips. The whips keep track of votes for and against bills, and they try to "whip up" support for their party.

Chapter 6

GET INVOLVED NOW!

Do you think you might want to run for office someday? It's never too early to start! Read local and national political news stories. What is happening in these stories that interests you? Are there specific politicians you like?

Be present! Attend political rallies and city council or school board meetings to explore issues that are important in your community. Visit local politicians at their offices or at town hall meetings. Talk with people who have similar or different opinions from your own. Learn why specific issues are important to them. By learning about leadership now, you'll set yourself up for success in the future.

The White House has sponsored events inviting kids to the nation's capital, including a science fair, an Hour of Code, and a Kids' State Dinner.

YOUNG LEADERS

In 1818 John Henry Eaton became the youngest senator at the age of 28. Although the Constitution says a senator must be at least 30, no one asked him his age. Armistead Mason (1816) and Henry Clay (1806) were also under 30 when they were sworn in. Rush Holt was elected at 29 years and 4 months old, and could not take his seat until after he turned 30 in 1935. Former Delaware Senator Joe Biden was sworn in at 30 years, 1 month, and 14 days of age.

Joe Biden
(1942–   )

GLOSSARY

amendment (uh-MEND-muhnt)—a change made to a law or a legal document

appropriations (uh-pro-pree-AY-shuhns)—the congressional power to collect taxes and authorize spending federal government money

bribe (BRIBE)—giving money or gifts to persuade someone to do something, especially something illegal or dishones

cloture (klo-CHUR)—a procedure for ending a debate and taking a vote

constituents (kuhn-STIT-choo-uhnts)—the people who live and vote in a Congress member's home state or district

Democratic Party (de-muh-KRA-tik PAR-tee)—one of the two major parties in the United States; Democrats are viewed as more progressive, supporting social and economic equality. They also believe the government should use more control with the economy, but less in private affairs.

executive branch (ig-ZE-kyuh-tiv BRANCH)—the branch of government that makes sure the laws are obeyed

federal (FED-ur-uhl)—relating to the U.S. government

filibuster (FILL-uh-bus-ter)—an effort to prevent action by making a long speech

impeach (im-PEECH)—charge an elected official with a serious crime; it can result in removal from office

judicial branch (joo-DISH-uhl BRANCH)—the part of government that explains laws

legislative branch (LEJ-iss-lay-tiv BRANCH)—the part of government that passes bills that become laws

legislator (LEJ-is-lay-tor)–a person elected to make or propose laws

majority party (muh-JOR-uh-tee PAR-tee)—the party whose members make up more than half of the total membership of the group

minority party (MI-noh-ruh-tee PAR-tee)—the party whose members make up less than half of the total membership of the group

nominate (NOM-uh-nate)—name someone as a candidate for a government position

pension (PEN-shuhn)—money paid regularly to people who have retired from work

Republican Party (ri-PUHB-lik-uhn PAR-tee)—one fo the two major parties in the United States; Republicans believe in conservative social policies, low taxes, and believe the government should stay out of the economy.

treaty (TREE-tee)—a formal agreement between groups or nations

READ MORE

Goodman, Susan E. *See How They Run: Campaign Dreams, Election Schemes, and the Race to the White House.* New York: Bloomsbury, 2019.

Rechner, Amy. *U.S. Government Behind the Scenes.* North Mankato, MN.: Compass Point Books, 2019.

Sobel, Syl. *How the U.S. Government Works and How It All Comes Together to Make a Nation.* Hauppauge, New York: Barron's, 2019.

INTERNET SITES

Learn About the Senate
https://www.senate.gov/reference/Index/Learning_About_Senate.htm

United States Senate Youth Program
https://ussenateyouth.org/

U.S. Capitol Visitor Center, The U.S. Senate
https://www.visitthecapitol.gov/about-congress/us-senate

CRITICAL THINKING QUESTIONS

1. Name the three branches of government. Describe the main responsibility of each. How do they work together?
2. Where do senators get ideas for new bills? Explain the steps to make a bill a law.
3. Research your state's senator. What beliefs do you have in common? Where do you disagree?

INDEX